SEO

Easy Search Engine Optimization

Your Step-By-Step Guide to a Sky-High Search Engine Ranking and Never Ending Traffic

Felix Alvaro

Acknowledgments

Firstly, I want to thank God for giving me the knowledge and inspiration to put this informative book together. I also want to thank my parents, my brothers and my partner Silvia for their support.

Table of Contents

Introduction

Hi there! Congratulations on acquiring this guide.

You have taken a very important step to taking your site to new heights. Literally. What you are about to learn in this guide are the steps you need to take to achieve a sky-high ranking and drive endless traffic to your site. Thousands of people today are creating amazing websites with awesome content/products but are struggling to get it out there and are not getting the flow of traffic that they want. It seems like Google doesn't care about them or their site. That's because they do not know the *right* strategies they need to take to make their site stand out and be placed above their competition. The internet is full of 'SEO gurus' that provide 'unknown secrets' for getting your site ranking over-night. Most of the time, those 'secrets' will either get you nowhere, or get you penalized and in worse shape than you were in before.

That's why this guide has been created. My name is Felix and I am an Online Marketer, Entrepreneur and Investor with the mission to help other aspiring Entrepreneurs, Web-Developers, Online-Marketers, Bloggers, etc. achieve their goals. In this guide, I will be teaching you proven SEO methods to help you to achieve the online success you desire.

This guide will only focus on the strategies that actually work, leaving out the tricks, schemes and stunts. Taking SEO seriously is vital. You will enable your website, brand and cause to be seen and help more people. Being seen by more people will allow you to help more people and get you better results, more success and establish the authority of your site and brand. It is a cycle of success.

Many businesses, charities, and organizations these days, have realised that one of the best investments they can make for their website in terms of marketing and advertising is putting more focus on SEO and getting their site higher on the search engine result pages. The returns they will get from a slight increase in rankings can be huge. To give you an idea, the first site on Google gets 42% of the traffic and the 3rd site gets 8% of the traffic. That is a significant difference in traffic and surely a huge difference in revenue.

By you investing in this guide, you too are making a big investment in your brand and cause. In this guide, I am going to give you information on all the strategies you need to implement to boost your ranking, increase your visibility, get your traffic numbers up and enjoy greater success. Whether you are using WordPress or coding, this guide is for you. I have put it together in a step-by-step format so that it will be easy for you to follow each instruction, no matter what your knowledge of SEO is. Everything is broken down properly. The language used is jargon-free and I have also included clear images so that you have a visual illustration of what you should be doing.

I can promise you that if you follow the steps I have laid out for you in this simple guide, you will without a doubt achieve greater online success. The time for you to take your website to the next level, is now. So without further ado, let's get started right away.

In the first chapter, I will be teaching you more about SEO, how it works, how search engines work and then I will be taking you through the first step you need to take to get your site ranking on search engines. I will be covering the functionality of search engines and the first step you need to take to get your site ranking.

Let's get to it!

Chapter One: Introduction to SEO

What is SEO and How does it Work?

Search Engine Optimization or SEO for short, does exactly what the name says it does; optimize websites for search engines. It combines a number of different strategies, procedures and actions that are used to increase website traffic organically (in other words, unpaid) by tactically placing the website in the highest possible position in search engine results.

Ranking highly on search engines is very important as the majority of web traffic comes from the largest search engines (Google, Yahoo and Bing). Nowadays, the majority of web users use search engines as their main point of contact to websites as search engines group all the possible, different and most relevant options on one page just like a super powerful yellow-pages book.

So if you rank high on these search engines, your website will get more targeted traffic that will be more exposure for your brand image, business, product or cause. In this guide, I am going to be covering all the basic principles you need to implement to flood your website with visitors and in return, achieve your website's desired objective.

How do Search Engines Operate?

Now, the key here is the high ranking in the search engine, so it would be fair to say that the search engines play the main role in the success of our websites. Therefore, I think it is right to assume that understanding how they operate is a fundamental point. Below, I am going to explain in very simple terms, how a search engine works.

In a nutshell, search engines have three main tasks: Crawling, Indexing and Providing Answers (aka 'Searching').

1. Crawling and Indexing

A beautiful thing about the internet is the billions and billions of nuggets of information available to us at a click of a mouse. For the most part, the days of spending hours in the library, going through books and files to find the answer to a simple question are now gone. Today, research time has been reduced to milliseconds through easy access to information on our laptops and smartphones and most importantly, due to the power of search engines.

"How do they do it?"

Well they use 'Crawlers'. Crawlers or 'Spiders' are automated robots created by search engines to collect data from billions of web pages, pdf files, photo files, the whole lot. These bots are sent on spy missions to go through all the data flying all over the internet and their job is to read the code, look out for the most important indicators of the page's content (title, subtitle, meta tags, etc.) and store this information as well as its location.

2. Providing Answers

The overwhelming amount of data that is stored in numerous worldwide databases is then processed in milliseconds to provide answers to internet browsers searching for an answer, particular file, topic, etc.

When someone searches for something, the search engine uses the indexed data to give the searcher the best result possible. The crawlers go back into action and bring forth information that is popular and with relevant words, titles, tags, etc. that best match the keywords searched.

This is a very simplistic explanation but nevertheless gives you a very good understanding of the functions of search engines. I must say that nowadays, search engines have become smarter and have more complex algorithms where only the fittest websites survive.

A question people commonly ask is:

"Why do I need to do anything at all then?"

or

"Why don't the search engines that are so advanced, take care of everything for me?"

Well, as advanced and as powerful as they are, search engines still require some assistance from you. There are thousands of new websites going live every day and many in your target niche, so it is in your best interest to make the job as easy as possible for the search engines and ensure they collect as much information about your site as possible.

By taking the right actions and optimizing your website the right way, you are giving yourself a massive advantage over other websites in your target market and attracting thousands of visitors to your website, versus the competition. If you fail to take SEO seriously, you are literally limiting your success and missing out on huge opportunities.

For this reason, it must be your number one purpose to understand all you can about this topic and to put the information in this book into practice so that you may achieve a sky-high ranking and never-ending traffic for website. With SEO, you will help the engines locate and provide your content to relevant users.

SEO is about fixing certain areas of your site. We will discuss those areas in the following chapter. The goal is simply:

Number One: To increase your position on search engine results, preferably to the first page

Number Two: To have our content reach as many relevant users as possible

Now, I will say that you should not create a website that focuses solely on giving the search engines what they want, but you should focus on improving your website and giving visitors a better opportunity to find your amazing content. Combine what you are going to learn here with amazing content and you will most definitely succeed. We will go into more detail on the importance of high-quality content in a later chapter.

Apart from search engines, there are also search websites called directories. These websites are similar to search engines, as they allow users to find particular services by searching, however the way they display sites is different. Like we discussed, search engines use algorithms and bots that go all over the net looking for webpages that match particular searches, but with directories, everything is done manually. They have a team of people that search through the internet looking to find new websites and that are also responsible for reviewing websites that would like to be featured on their site. People doing this manually means that users will be assured that the websites featured are of high quality.

Though less popular, directories can still be a good source of traffic for you, but just bear in mind that your website will have to stand out immensely from others to be featured. Also, you may have to pay an administrative-fee to be featured on a directory site.

The First Step to Ranking in Search Engines

As you can probably begin to tell from the last few points, SEO is not rocket science. There are a few components that will get a website ranking high and I have dropped a few hints already. However, before we discuss in detail what those tactics are, we must first get your website in the search engines and give you an extra boost by helping the search engines help you.

If you followed the simple step-by-step instructions in my **best-selling** book:

http://amzn.to/1VHtxZi

"WORDPRESS: Simple WordPress Guide to Create an Attractive Website or Blog from Scratch, Step-By-Step", then you have probably already setup a well-functioning website that has an appealing appearance and that is full of relevant and original content. If you have not, don't worry! I will be covering that in the later chapters! Now it is time to actually submit our website to the search engines to make the ranking process quicker.

The first step to ranking on search engines is to manually submit your website to different search engines! Manually submitting is recommended as it will less likely mark your site as spam when appearing in search engine results. The more search

13

engines you submit your site to, the easier it can be with ranking in the results. For this example, we will focus on Google as it is responsible for 67% of the world's searches, but we will be addressing different search engines throughout the book as they are important too. There are different ways of submitting to search engines depending on what kind of content you are offering. For website submission, the simplest way is by submitting your URL.

Here Are 3 Simple Steps:

1. Visit http://www.google.com/addurl. You will need a Gmail account to continue. If you do not have one, it's recommended you create one)

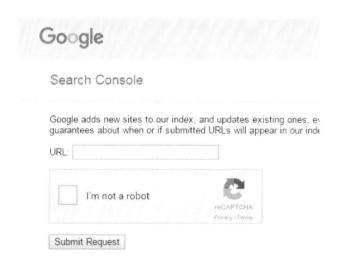

2. Simply copy and paste the URL you created for your website into the section marked 'URL.' Be sure to

include the whole link so it will appear as http://www.YourURLHere.com/ in the box.

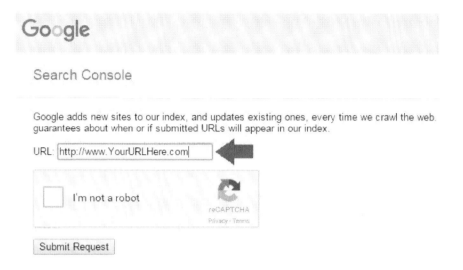

3. The last step here should be to click the verification icon and then hit *Submit Request*!

Your website has been submitted to Google search engines! You are on your way to getting your site out there! So far so good!

As mentioned before, it is best to do numerous submissions of your site's URL to as many search engines as possible to get maximum exposure for your brand. For other search engines to submit your site to visit:

www.fast-traffic-seo.blogspot.com

This site includes several search engines that you can pick and choose from, as well listing different submission techniques for those search engines!

Another great website to find the best free search engines and directories to submit to is:

So your site has been submitted! Are we done? No, not quite! Even though we have now submitted our site, there is no guarantee when or where your website will appear in the search engine results since it will take a day or two before it is completely submitted, but even then it's unlikely to be ranked very high. Nevertheless, this is great progress! The next chapter is very, very important. I will go into the world of *keywords*. Keywords link your website to a particular search and doing this correctly is the foundation to successful search engine rankings. Stay tuned!

Chapter Two: The Importance of Keywords

Keywords Are Key

Keywords are the most important ingredient to successful SEO campaigns. They are the vehicle that directs a specific visitor to your website. Like I mentioned early on in the first chapter, Google will connect a search to an answer first and foremost based on the keywords. If the keywords or topics are not the same, then the result would be irrelevant. It is quite fair to say that, if you do not exercise what I am going to teach you in this chapter, your other efforts will not benefit you as they should. Doing this correctly is not very challenging and it solely requires a few tactics in analysing the best terms to rank for.

In a nutshell, you want to target keywords that:

- Have low competition
- Have high popularity
- Are relevant to your site and the content, products, and/or services you are offering

Short Tail vs. Long Tail

Once upon a time, there was a world where one could simply dominate a one-to-two-word market, or *short-tail*, for example, "food recipes". The competition was so low and the level of difficulty to rank was very minimal if you knew what you were doing. Those days are pretty much gone and now it is those that learn to find other more specific niche markets and dominate them that succeed. The new market requires you to go after *long-tail* keywords.

Long-tail keywords are 3-5 word phrases that target a specific market. For example, with the "food recipes" example, trying to rank for 'food recipes' alone would be both very challenging and unwise. You would be attracting people that could be searching for various things with those keywords and you wouldn't really be segmenting the right market for your site. You want to target a specific group of people in that 'recipes' market, so you could rank for "Vegan Recipes" instead, as that is more narrowed down and would attract targeted traffic to your webpage.

You could get even more specific such as "Vegan Recipes for bodybuilders". Now that is very specific and will most likely give you more opportunities to rank high and provide the market with what it wants. Of course, you would have to do your keyword research to ensure that it is a profitable and popular niche and we will discuss keyword analysis in a second.

How to Find the Best Keywords

To find good long-tail keywords you want to firstly, get out a pen and paper or open up a Word doc and start writing down:

- Describe the content of your site
- Keywords that are relevant to your market
- Write down the short-tail keywords people are most likely to search when looking for that type of content
- Write down synonyms for those keywords
- Write down at least 10 keywords/phrases

Quick Tip: If you are selling a product or service, it is a very good idea to rank for 'buying words'. Buying words are additional keywords that you will add to your primary keyword to target a user with purchasing intent. For example, if you are selling recipe books, instead of just ranking for 'vegan recipes', you should rank for 'vegan recipe books', or 'buy vegan recipe books', etc. The additional words like 'book' and 'buy' in these examples will be typed by people looking to potentially make a purchase. It is best to target those people as they may be ready to pull out their credit card, instead of having people that are simply looking for free information. Regardless, check which combination of buying words together with your keywords that are most popular and make the most sense for your offer.

Here is a list of the best 'buying words' you can use:

- Bargain + (product) like "bargain books"
- Budget
- Buy + (product) this is the best one
- Buy + (product/service) + online
- Order + (product/service)
- Purchase + (product/service)
- Best Price + (product/service)
- Best reviews of + (product/service)
- Cheap + (product/service)
- Cheapest + (product/service)
- Low price + (product/service)
- Low cost + (product/service)
- Affordable + (product/service)
- Clearance + (product/service)
- Discounted + (product/service)
- (product/service) + For Sale
- Good price for + (product/service)
- Inexpensive + (product/service)
- Good value + (product/service
- Reduced + (product/service
- Best + (product/service
- Top + (product/service) + to buy
- Top + (product/service) + online
- Where can I buy + (product/service name)
- Where to buy + (product/service name)
- Where to find + (product/service name)
- (product/service name) + for cheap
- (product/service) for sale
- (product/service) for sale online
- (product/service) under $50
- (product/service) + discount
- (product/service name) + on sale
- How to + (product/service)

Analysing Your Keywords

You are then going to take your list of keywords over to my favourite keyword tool: *Google AdWords Keyword Tool*.

This tool will provide you with quality information on the best keywords to use, an estimate in search volume and trends in popularity over time to show whether this is a growing or declining term or even topic.

How to Use the Keyword Tool

Using this tool is very easy and I am going to run through the simple steps:

1. Create or sign in to your Gmail account. (To create one visit www.Gmail.com.)
2. Visit this URL: http://adwords.google.com.
3. Enter your information or simply click '*Skip the guided set-up*' (recommended).

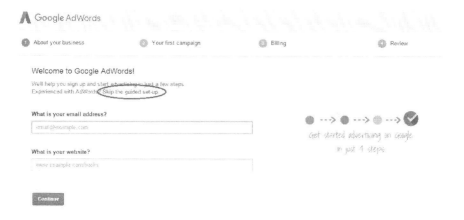

4. Create your AdWords Account and then click '*Save and Continue*'.

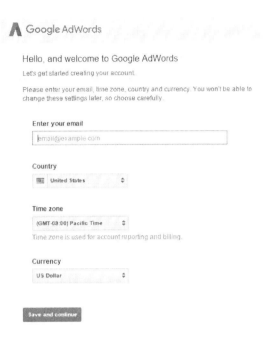

5. You should arrive in the AdWords Home Page.

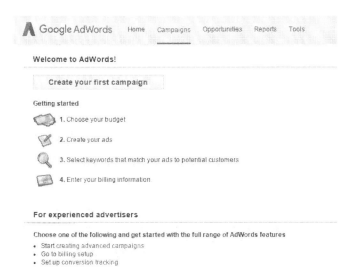

6. Click on the *Tools* tab and then select '*Keyword Planner*'.

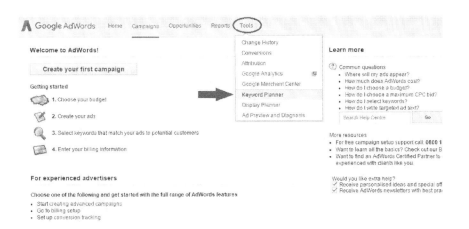

7. Then you want to click on *'Search for new Keywords using a phrase, website or category'*.

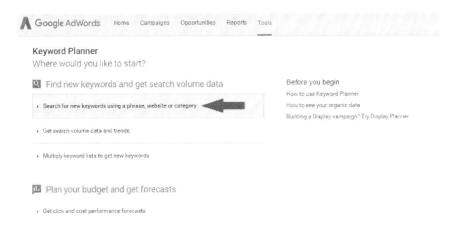

8. Enter your primary keyword or phrase in the *'Your product or service'* box.

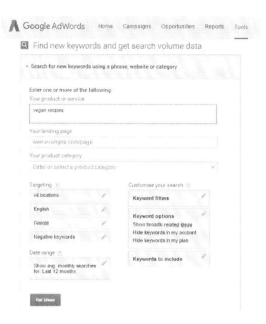

9. You then want to change the location of your search to the location of your target market. This is because you will most likely only rank high on one of the Google versions (For example: Google.com). If you are getting global search volume data, then it will not be accurate in accordance with what your market is searching for in their version of Google. So in the *Location* box, enter the relevant country or countries.

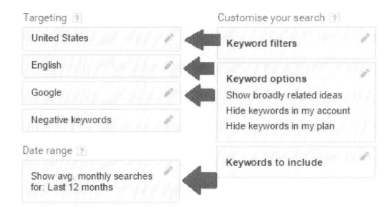

Once that is done, ensure the language is set to *'English'* or the language relevant to your target market and also make sure you have *Google* as the source of the data we are collecting.

Also, ignore all the other tabs apart from the 'date range' which should be set for a 12-month period.

10. Hit 'Get Ideas'.

11. Here is what the search result page will look like:

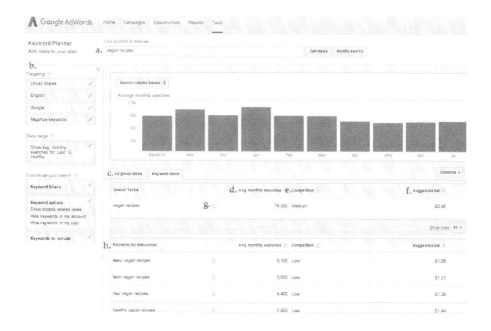

a) **Keyword Search-** Can be changed with a new keyword at any time. Press '*Get ideas*' to search

b) **Targeting-** The criteria we set for the search, can be updated at any time.

c) **Group Ideas-** A group of keywords that you can purchase for ad campaigns. We want to click on '*Keyword ideas*' to view keyword search volume.

d) **Average Monthly Searches-** Estimated search volume on a monthly basis, click on it to filter results based on high to low, or low to high search volume.

e) **Competition-** Shows the level of competition for the bidding of that particular keyword. This is not supposed to be an indication of the difficulty to rank on Google, but it can still give you an idea of how popular the term is for web-marketers. It is fair to assume that a higher bid price could mean higher demand for ads on that particular keyword.

f) **Suggested Bid** (ignore)- Bid estimate for an advert.

g) **Trends Icon**- Will show you the trend in search volume for the last 12 months. Good for analysing whether the term or even topic is growing or declining in popularity.

h) **Keyword (by relevance)**- Shows other relevant keywords. If you use it as a filter, it will show you the most relevant keywords matching your search. Great way to find more possible terms to target.

12. Enter all the keywords you wrote down previously in the search box and hit *Get ideas.*

13. Go through the keyword ideas and see which terms are both relevant to your topic as well as reasonably popular.

14. I would aim mainly for long tail keywords as those will be more narrowed down and will give you a better chance to rank highly, even if there is a lower search volume.

These are the steps to using the Google keyword tool. By now, you should have a good list of good keywords that you can rank for, but there is just one more step I must cover.

Analysing the Competition

Now you will need to analyse how competitive each keyword is as you want to go for a keyword that is not over-competitive and that gives you a chance to outrank sites to land yourself on the first page. The best way to analyse this is to enter each keyword in Google and go through the first couple of pages to see which websites you are up against.

Bear in mind that when you do a search, there are many websites that rank for a keyword they are not trying to rank for it. Those websites, as well as badly optimized ones, will give you the opportunity to outrank and be on top.

When you are looking through the sites, the things you should pay attention to are listed below. Now, many of the factors I am about to list below will be completely new to you, but my aim is to plant the terms in your mind here in Chapter Two and as you read the rest of this guide, you will begin to understand SEO better and will have the knowledge and capability to beat your competition. I recommend that once you have read the book, return to this part of the chapter to refresh your mind on the way to analyse the competition as it will make better sense to you.

Here you are:
1. URL- Is the keyword in the domain name/URL?
2. Page Titles (Title tags) - Is the site using the relevant keywords in the title?
3. Headers- Is the keyword in the header?
4. Can you spot the keyword in the actual content?
5. Is the content relevant to the keyword?

31

6. Is the content high-quality and does it seem like it has been written by an 'authority' on the subject?
7. Are there other posts on the website relating to the same topics?
8. Do you see any social media buttons?
9. Repeat this process until you know which keywords are worth pursuing.

Now, I am going to show you the best tools to quickly gather this information.

1. SEOQUAKE

SEOQuake is a toolbar extension available for Google Chrome, Firefox, Opera and Safari. This tool will allow you to analyse your competitor's site in a matter of seconds. When on a search engine result pages, it will display a small bar at the bottom of the search result that will provide you with a lot of important data such as:

- **The PageRank-** PageRank is an algorithm that scores the importance of a site from 0-10 based on the number of sites that are linking to them. Every link is like a 'vote' that added up gives a page a PageRank score.
- **Search Engine Index-** The index will show you the number of pages that are indexed and stored by the

particular search engine. (Available for Google, Yahoo, Bing and Yandex)

- **Alexa Rank-** Alexa is the leading web traffic data and analytics site. The Alexa Rank ranks sites by popularity and traffic. This tool will show you how stable a website is and will give you an idea of the efforts required to overtake it.

- **Keyword Density** (when you open a page) - The percentage of times each keyword (or particular keyword) appears throughout the page.

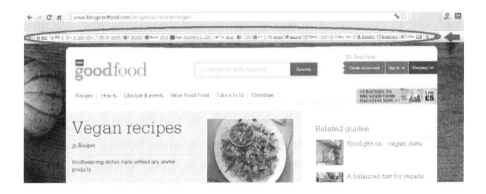

You can also edit the tool to display the information that you want, which can allow you to view information like the number of Facebook Likes the page has, the number of tweets and a lot of other awesome data. To edit your parameters, click the SEOQuake icon on your browser's toolbar > Click the settings icon > Preferences > Parameters and then simply tick the Parameters you would like to view.

2. MOZBAR

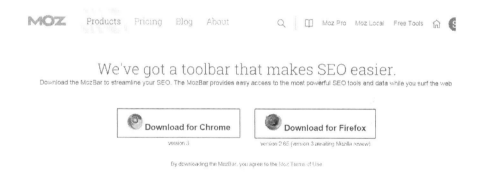

MozBar is also another amazing extension that will also give you vital information such as;

- **Page's Authority Rank**- Page Authority is similar to PageRank. It gives a website a rank based on its popularity and links. Page Authority may even be a better indicator of a site's power as it is updated monthly, in comparison with the 3 months it takes for PageRank to be updated. The lower the rank, the easier it is to outrank them.
- **Number of Backlinks to that Particular Page**- Backlinks are links from other sites to your site. They are seen as a major indicator of a site's popularity by search engines and play a big role on a site's rank. The fewer high-quality backlinks your competition has, the easier it will be to outrank that page.
- **Domain Authority Rank**- Domain Authority quantifies the power or 'authority' your website has by giving it a ranking between 0-100.
- **Number of Backlinks to the Entire Site**- The number of backlinks to the entire site will show you how established the site is.

You need to get access to all the information you have to create a basic and easy to setup an account with Moz. When you open a page, you will also be able to see more cool info like a spam score, social media activity and my personal favourite feature, *The Page Analysis* tool which will show you the page's URL, the page title, the meta description, the meta keywords, Header tags and more.

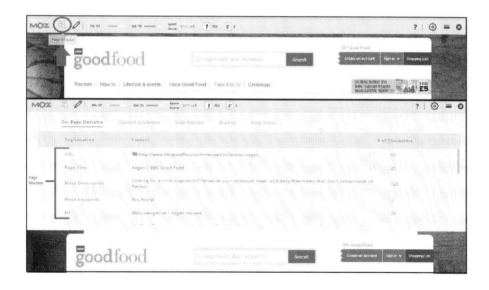

By combining these two tools, you will gather information that will enable you to determine which keywords you should be ranking for. Remember that you should be turning to long tail keywords as those will present you with less, or easier keywords to outrank your competition. However, don't be surprised or demotivated if you see quite few sites with a high PageRank, Domain Authority rankings, many links and so on in the first page. This is normal. Focus on the 'weaker' sites you can outrank. See if they are properly optimizing their site by including keywords in their titles, headers, images, etc. and if they are doing it correctly.

I will also add that when you do make the right changes which I am going to run you through in the next few chapters, don't expect to outrank sites immediately. Give search engines time and allow the process to run smoothly. Be sure to manage your expectations and be patient.

Great work! You are learning a lot.

Chapter Three: On page Optimization

In this chapter, I am going to show you how to correctly optimize your website on page. I am going to show the 3 most important tags you should add to your site and how to implement them correctly, step by step.

Now that we have a good list of keywords we can target, we want to begin using them in optimizing our website. We are going to cover all the changes that you have to make, or improve, on your actual website so that it ranks high. Pay close attention to what I am going to cover in this chapter and implement it as soon as possible.

Title Tags

The first tag we are going to cover is the Title Tags. The title tags are very important since they are used by search engines to determine the content on a web page by reading the keywords that are placed. When you search for something on Google for instance, the blue title of the link is the title tag.

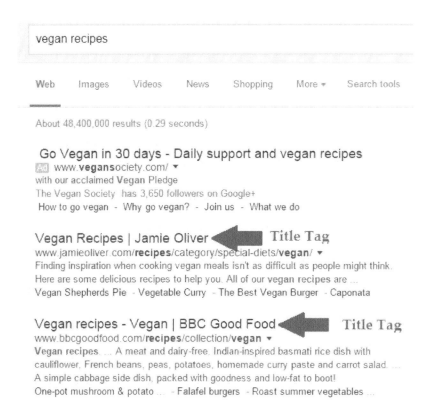

If you remember carefully, this is one of the things I told you to look out for on your competitors' websites as it shows you whether they are directly targeting that particular keyword and whether that is the main focus of their page.

This should be the first place where you should include your keywords.

Now, every title should be different in accordance to the content of the page. Here are some great tips on how to properly structure your title:

1. First of all, make it <u>readable.</u> Don't simply try to stuff keywords. People are more likely to click on a link that has an aesthetically attractive title.
2. Try to place your keyword as close to the <u>beginning of the title</u> as possible. Search engines read and place weight on words from left to right, however, be sure to take the advice I just gave you and make it make sense
3. Ideally <u>55 characters is best,</u> 70 characters is the maximum.
4. Leave the <u>branding until the end</u>. This goes hand-in-hand with point number 2. You want your keywords to be the first words in the title so leave your name until the end unless your brand is the main term people are searching for. Then you would want to place it at the start of the title.

If you look back at the image I showed you previously, you will see that the first 2 search results are targeting the keyword 'vegan recipes'. They included the keyword in their title tag and not only that, but they ensured having those keywords as the first words of the title and their own branding was left to the end (Jamie Oliver in the first search result and BBC in the second).

Great stuff!

Now that you understand what the title tag is, you understand its purpose and what it should contain, let's move on to the practical steps of adding a title tag.

We will start with <u>WordPress users.</u> If you are using code please skip this part!

For WordPress users:

1. Install the 'Yoast SEO' Plugin (previously called WordPress SEO by Yoast). This is one of my favourite all-time plugins, as I mentioned in my WordPress guide. (http://amzn.to/1VHtxZi)

2. Once the plugin is installed, simply create your page/post or open up the editor of the particular page you want to add a title to.

3. Scroll down past the text/content box and you will see the plugin's widget being displayed.

4. In the box titled *'Focus Keyword'*, enter the primary keyword (not the title) you are targeting for this entire page, which will tell the plugin that this is the keyword you want to focus on. The plugin will then have a list of places you need to include your keyword in to fully optimize your post or page. (Title, Heading, URL, Content and Meta Description will be discussed next.)

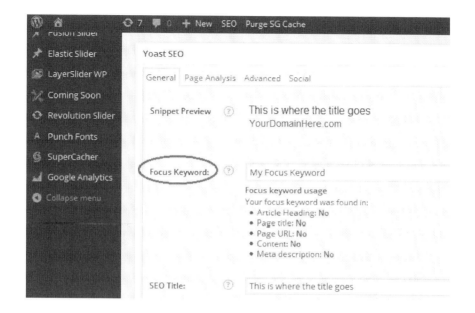

5. Create an aesthetically attractive title with the focus keyword as close to the beginning as possible (whilst making sense). Also, do not use the keyword in the title <u>more than once</u>, if possible! (I will cover more on title and headline writing in the final chapter!).

6. Enter it in the SEO Title box

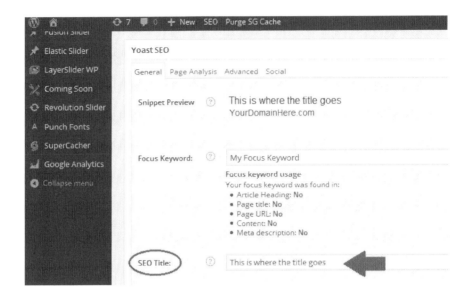

7. Done!

Now for all my coding masters! (WordPress Users May Skip)

Download The Kompozer HTML editor.

(Download Kompozer viisit; http://www.kompozer.net/)

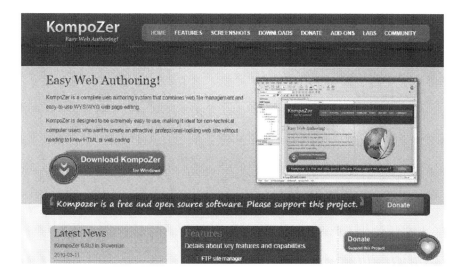

1. Open Kompozer.

2. Open the HTML source link of your site.

HTML Website
Firefox HTML Document
257 KB

3. Click Source at the bottom of the page.

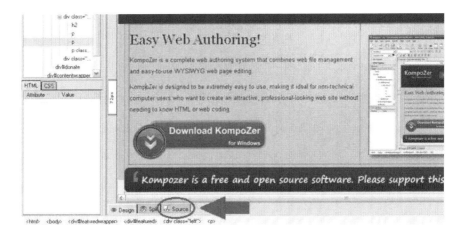

4. Within the *<head>* tags enter: *<title> You Keyword Rich Title Goes Here </title>*. Your <head> tags should be near the top of your HTML coding and should look something like this:

```
 1.  <!DOCTYPE html PUBLIC "-//W3C//DTD HTML 4.01//EN" "http://www.w3.org/TR/html4/strict.dtd">
 2.  <html>
 3.  <head>
 4.    <meta content="text/html; charset=ISO-8859-1"
 5.    http-equiv="content-type">
 6.    <title>Your Keyword Rich Title Tag Here</title>
 7.  </head>
 8.  <body>
 9.  <br>
10.  </body>
11.  </html>
```

5. Done!

Well done! You have just created your first search engine optimized and keyword optimized title using Yoast SEO for WordPress, or Kompozer for HTML coding!

Great progress!

Now let's move on to another very important element in on-page optimization. This key ingredient is called:

Header Tags

The second tag, but just as important and another great way to optimize your web-pages is to use header tags in your posts.

Header Tags are simply 'bolded' titles and subtitles (headings and subheadings) on your actual page. These 'bolded' words attract search engine bots by showing them headings containing information about the topic of your web-page. They then match the keywords in the heading with the content displayed on the page, much like title tags.

49

Search engines also see Header Tags as an additional usability boost as users can immediately distinguish the material discussed in your content. Good usability is highly valued by search engines.

This then gives us the opportunity to include our target keyword!

A H1 Tag on a Blog Post

There are usually 6 heading tags, with the h1 tag carrying the most weight and most relevant to the search engines, down to h6 tag being the least effective heading.

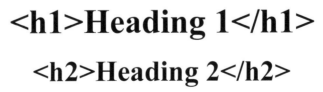

<h1>Heading 1</h1>
<h2>Heading 2</h2>

\<h3\>Heading 3\<h3/\>

\<h4\>Heading 4\<h4\>

\<h5\>Heading 5\</h5\>

\<h6\>Heading 6\</h6\>

My advice is to always use the h1 tag for the main title of the page or blog post, followed by the h2 tag for the subtitle and the h3 tag for the second subtitle. Just remember to place your keyword in all the tags, without overdoing it of course, and also it is advisable to not use more than one of each tag per page.

Now that you understand the use of Header Tags, I will show you how to include them on your website:

We will start with WordPress (Coders, please skip):

This is very, very easy to do with WordPress.

1. Create a new page or post or edit the page you wish to add the heading to.
2. Create your content as normal.

3. Highlight the phrase you want to make into a header.

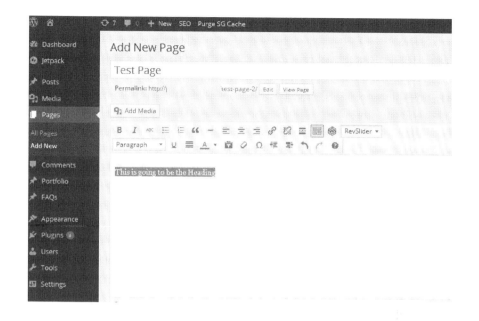

4. Click the paragraph drop-down box on the left hand-side of your toolbar.

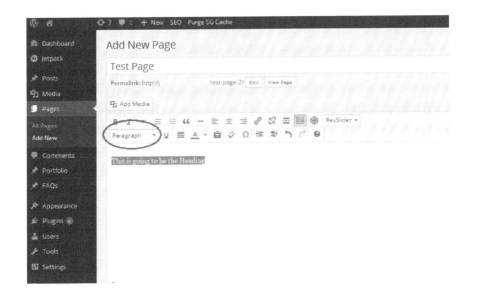

5. If you cannot see the paragraph toolbar, simply click on 'Toolbar Toggle' to display the additional tools.

6. Select the Heading you wish to apply it to.

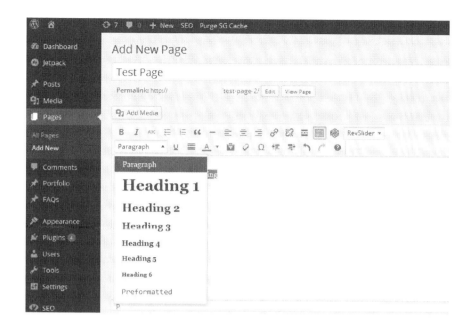

7. Click *Publish* or *Update*.

8. Done!

For the Coding Senseis!

It's very easy to add the Header Tag. Hopefully you have installed Kompozer as I recommended in the previous step. If you didn't, you can download it visit http://www.kompozer.net/. Here we are:

1. Open Kompozer to edit your site.
2. Click on the text style drop-down menu.

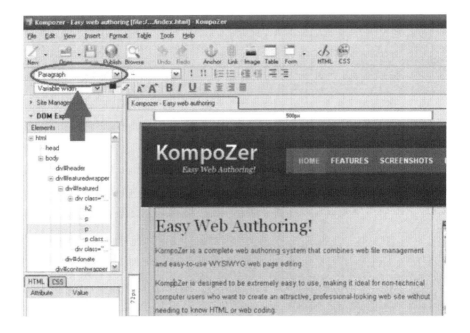

3. It will give the options of 'Heading1' up to 'Heading6'.

56

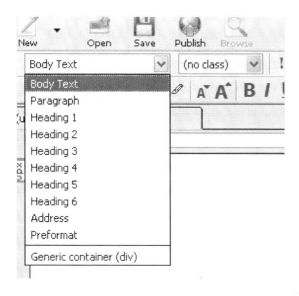

4. Choose your header tag and remember to include your keyword where relevant.

5. Done!

Awesome! We are making crucial steps. Now let's keep moving. Next, we will talk about the third very important factor tag: Meta Tags.

Meta Tags

Finally, Meta Tags are also something to consider when doing your on page optimization. They are used to summarise information on a web site and provide search engines with additional data. There are many different meta tags, but over the years many have been rejected by search engines and others simply aren't as effective as they once were. Still, there is a particular tag that I recommend you use and that is called a *Meta Description Tag.*

Meta Description

In a few words, a meta description literally provides search engines with a short description of the content of your web page. Search engines will sometimes use this description as a snippet of your web content just below your link on the search engine's results page.

You can easily write a meta description, which I will show you how to do shortly, but the reason why I said search engines 'sometimes use this' is because occasionally the search engine creates its own description out of the content on your actual page.

A good way around this is to actually have the description you choose, written on the page.

Nonetheless, go for it and write your own short description. See it as a point of contact with potential viewers and as an opportunity for you to further sell them the benefits of clicking on the page. Don't go overboard. Keep it simple and to the point.

You can also include your primary keywords in your description. These keywords won't boost your ranking but will be bolded or highlighted when included in the search, calling more attention to your search result. If you look at the google search result screenshot that I displayed previously, you will notice that the keyword 'vegan recipes' is highlighted in the meta description.

If my site was about 'Vegan Recipes for Bodybuilders', a good short description might be:

"Find delicious, low-fat and easy vegan recipes for bodybuilders perfect for your workout routine! Learn to prepare simple protein-rich snacks or tasty dinners for guests, Look no further…"

This is a very simple example and I am sure you can do much better, but the main things are that I am selling them benefits on clicking on my site. In this example, the benefits are:

- "Delicious"- Everyone likes delicious food.
- "Low-fat"- Bodybuilders are very focused on their diet and body.
- "Easy"- If they are looking for recipes, then they are probably not very skilled cooks so simple is best.
- "Vegan recipes for bodybuilders"- My primary keywords highlighted will attract more clicks.
- "Protein"- A big problem for vegan bodybuilders is getting enough protein, so here I am addressing that problem and providing a solution in my description.
- "Snack" or "Dinner"- My site offers diversity and caters to all.

With your description, think about the problems your visitors may be encountering and think about what interests them. Doing this will entice more people to click and increase your traffic numbers significantly.

Now that we have covered what a meta description is, it's time to apply it!

For WordPress Users (Coders Kindly skip.)

You should by now have installed the plugin 'Yoast SEO'. If you have not, please install it now. Once that is done, follow these simple steps:

1. Add a new Page or Post or edit an existing Page or Post.
2. Scroll-down to the Yoast SEO widget.
3. You will see a 'Meta Description' box.

4. Enter your description (maximum 156 characters).

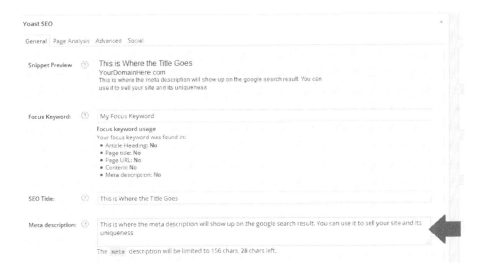

5. Ensure it looks fine in the *Snippet Preview* section in the widget, which is a preview of what your post will look like on Google's search results page.

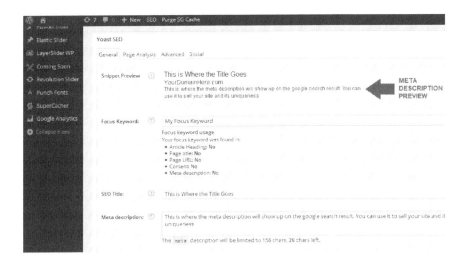

6. Click *Publish* or *Update*.

7. Done!

For All My Amazing Coders!

Again, here are the easy steps to add a meta description to your site;

1. Open Kompozer.
2. Open the HTML source link of your site.

3. Click Source at the bottom of the page.

4. In the *<head>* tags, edit the code with the following:

<head>
<meta name="description" content="Enter

Your Description Here!">
</head>

It should look like this:

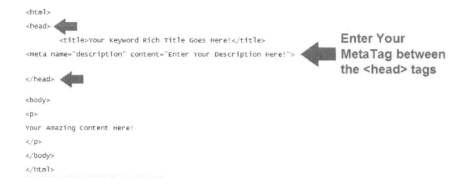

```
<html>
<head>
        <title>Your Keyword Rich Title Goes Here!</title>
<meta name="description" content="Enter Your Description Here!">
</head>
<body>
<p>
Your Amazing Content Here!
</p>
</body>
</html>
```

Enter Your MetaTag between the <head> tags

TIP: DO NOT waste your time with <u>meta</u> <u>keywords</u>. Meta keyword tags allow you to place a number of keywords you want to rank for without them actually appearing on your web page. However, I do not recommend using this tag as it will not help you at all. A few years ago, meta keywords were one of the most effective strategies, but because people were being unethical and stuffing irrelevant keywords, search engines changed their algorithms and now don't even consider meta keywords.

Other Important Places to Use Keywords

So we have now covered the use of keywords in the title, header tags and even meta descriptions. Now we are going to discuss their use in the actual content. I usually come across two extremes when it comes to keywords in the content:

1. Not using the right keywords at all.
2. Overusing the keywords.

Now both of the above are a problem. You must have your keywords in your content but you should avoid overdoing it.

When crawlers go through your site, they look to see patterns in the material you have published that tell them the 'true' themes of your content. The reason why some people don't include the right keywords in their content is because they are targeting keywords that do not relate to their topic. If you followed my steps so far, you should not be in this group.

Overusing keywords, or stuffing keywords in the content is the most common mistake and this mistake can cause you serious problems. If you are just throwing keyword around, search engines might think you are spamming and the consequences can be lethal.

It is very easy to avoid these problems. My advice is to include your targeted keyword in the first paragraph of content and in the last paragraph too. Don't try to force it and keep the material natural.

The percentage of times Google recommends using your primary keywords, is around 1-2% of your content. This is the Keyword Density that I had told you about at the end of Chapter Two. However, I will say that you shouldn't stress out if you are above this percentage as long as the keywords are mentioned naturally and are part of what you are talking about. In that case you have nothing to worry about.

Other places to include keywords:

- **URLs**- When choosing the URL for a new page or post, you can use the keywords that are relevant to that page or post to increase your ranking. (www.example.com/Include-Your-Keywords-Here). You should also look for this when examining your competitor's sites.
- **Image Tag**- Add a keyword to the HTML code of an image. For example: *<img src="File-Name-Including-Keyword.jpg" title="Title-Of-The-Image-Include-Primary-Keywords">*. These keywords are not visible on the page but will help your ranking.
- **Internal links**- When linking from one page to another, do not use images as the links but instead have text links that include keywords relevant to the page you're linking to. This is called 'Anchor Text' and is a simple strategy that gives you a nice boost on keyword optimization.

I am going to take this opportunity to say that varying your keywords is important. All these strategies that I have mentioned so far can really help catapult you to the top and the more times you use them, the better. To do this, use variations of your primary keywords. Look for synonyms and other ways of mentioning your primary keywords and topics. Then include those terms in subheading tags, in the code of images, in your content and so forth. To make this even more effective, use Google AdWords to find the most popular synonyms.

Tracking Your Site - Google Analytics

Knowing your numbers is essential. It will allow you to monitor your progress, see what is working and what is not working in your SEO efforts.

To help you, Google created an amazing tool called '*Google Analytics*'.

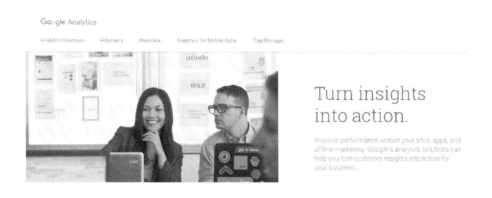

This website will allow you to see amazing information that can allow you to make the right changes to your site.

Here are just a few, basic examples of what Google Analytics can do:

- Provide you with accurate data on the <u>number</u> of visitors your site gets
- Show which <u>keywords</u> are attracting the most traffic to your website. This will enable you to see how your keywords are performing and enable you to know which keywords you should focus on.
- Give you information on which <u>sources</u> are directing the highest number of visitors to your site (which websites are directing viewers, which blogs, articles etc.). Crucial information!
- Show you the pages on your website people are <u>landing</u> on the most
- Show you the pages they are <u>leaving</u> from the most
- It will show you the <u>countries</u>/<u>locations</u> where people are accessing your site from and <u>much</u> <u>more</u>!

To access this information, visit http://www.google.com/analytics/ and sign in to your Gmail account or create a new account if you don't have one. (Visit Gmail.com to signup) Once you are in, you need to simply enter your site's information and then enter the 'tracking code' Google will provide you to your web pages.

In a couple of hours, you will be up and running!

If you are using **WordPress** (Coders please skip);

1. Install the *Google Analytics by Yoast* Plugin from your dashboard.

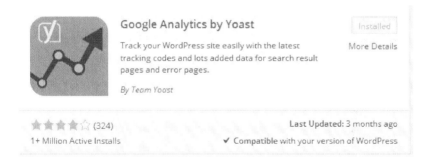

2. Hover over *Analytics* > Click on *Settings* on your WordPress Dashboard.

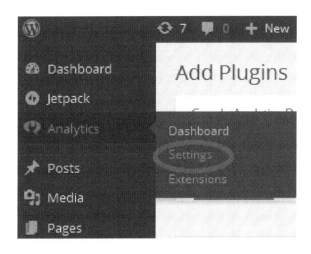

3. Click on *Authenticate with your Google Account.*

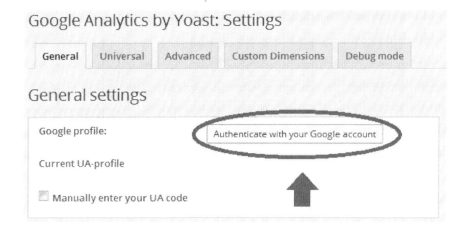

4. Sign-in with the same Google account you used for setting up Google Analytics.

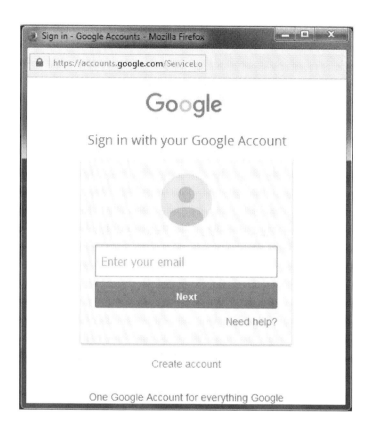

5. Click on *Allow*.

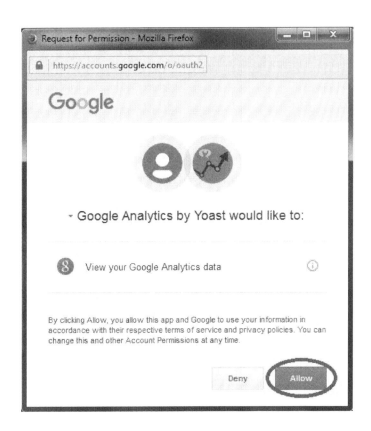

6. Copy the code that shows up, paste it in the box and click *Save Authentication Code.*

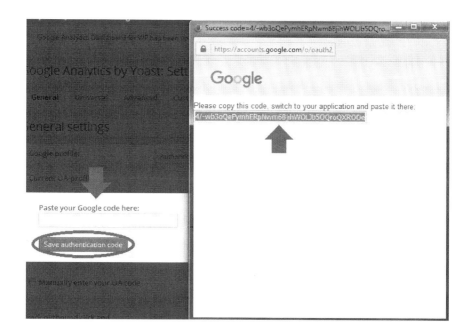

7. Select your site's UA code from the drop-down menu and then Click *Save Changes*.

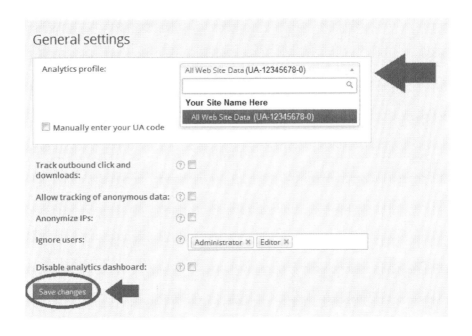

General settings

Analytics profile:	All Web Site Data (UA-12345678-0)
	Your Site Name Here
	All Web Site Data (UA-12345678-0)
☐ Manually enter your UA code	

Track outbound click and downloads: ⑦ ☐

Allow tracking of anonymous data: ⑦ ☐

Anonymize IPs: ⑦ ☐

Ignore users: ⑦ [Administrator ✕] [Editor ✕]

Disable analytics dashboard: ⑦ ☐

Save changes

8. Done! Now when you want to see the latest statistics for your site, simply Click on *Analytics* on your WordPress Dashboard.

If you are using Code;

1. Open your site in the Kompozer editor (or your HTML editor).
2. Click on Source at the bottom of the page.
3. Go to your Google Analytics page > Click the *Admin* tab > under *Property* select your site and then Click on *Tracking Info* > Click *Tracking Code.*

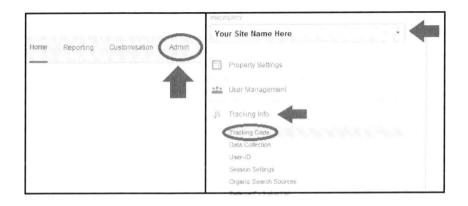

4. Copy your *Universal Analytics Tracking Code* (everything including *<script>* up until *</script>*.

5. Return to your HTML editor and paste the tracking code in the *<head>* tag of every single page you want to track.

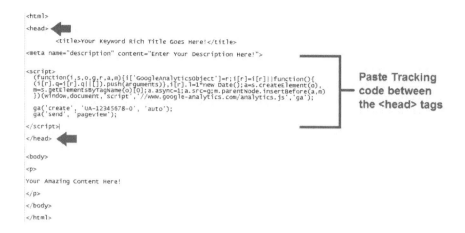

```
<html>
<head>
    <title>Your Keyword Rich Title Goes Here!</title>
<meta name="description" content="Enter Your Description Here!">

<script>
    (function(i,s,o,g,r,a,m){i['GoogleAnalyticsObject']=r;i[r]=i[r]||function(){
    (i[r].q=i[r].q||[]).push(arguments)},i[r].l=1*new Date();a=s.createElement(o),
    m=s.getElementsByTagName(o)[0];a.async=1;a.src=g;m.parentNode.insertBefore(a,m)
    })(window,document,'script','//www.google-analytics.com/analytics.js','ga');

    ga('create', 'UA-12345678-0', 'auto');
    ga('send', 'pageview');
</script>
</head>

<body>
<p>
Your Amazing Content Here!
</p>
</body>
</html>
```

Paste Tracking code between the <head> tags

6. Save and you are Done!

This data will allow you to monitor the performance of your optimization, as you will understand what does and doesn't work. Once you have tracked your site for a while, simply go back and make calculated improvements to the steps we have covered on the basis of the information you have received. Consistently tracking and improving your website will give you an advantage over the majority of your competitors, so do the best you can.

To learn more about Google Analytics, visit https://moz.com/blog/absolute-beginners-guide-to-google-analytics.

Wow! You have made so much progress and learnt a lot of valuable information. In this chapter we covered different on page optimization strategies. In the next chapter, we will discuss the second piece of the puzzle which is off-page optimization and how a few tactics can really boost your rank and increase the flow of traffic to your site. Stay tuned!

Chapter Four: Off page Optimization

While on page optimization dealt with clever changes to your actual site, off page optimization deals with strategies that should be implemented outside your website to boost your ranking and traffic. Some of the things I am going to discuss in this chapter, can be even more effective and powerful than what we have covered so far so please pay close attention.

Backlinks

The off page strategy I would like to start with is *Backlinking*.

Backlinking is essentially a link from another webpage that links to your site or post. These links can come from various places such as social media pages, blogs and all types of websites. Now that may sound very basic and it is, however it is very important from a search engine's point of view. In short, search engines see a large number of **QUALITY** links from other pages to your site as a sign of popularity, authority and relevance to a particular search query.

Also, getting trusted and quality sites to display links to yours is a bit more challenging than simply doing a few on page changes, so for this reason search engines see backlinks as good indicators of your site's real value.

Remember: <u>Never</u> pay for backlinks, period. They do more bad than good.

There are a few ways to get backlinks and we will cover those in a second. Before that, I want to make sure you are aware that not all backlinks are good and there are some key components that separate good quality links from poor ones.

First and foremost, the best backlinks come from **sites that are about the same topic** as yours. For instance, if there was a website about 'Vegan Dieting' that has a link to my 'Vegan Recipes' site, then that would be a relevant connection and be seen as a valuable link by the search engines, in comparison with a link from a website about technology for instance. I am sure you get the point.

Also, the **fewer outgoing links on that webpage the better** as the authority, trust and PageRank that flows from that site is divided equally to every website it links to. As a rough guideline, a higher quality backlink comes from a webpage that has 10 or less outgoing links on the same page that is linking to yours. This is just an ideal scenario so don't be too worried about it.

Now that we mentioned **PageRank** (PR), this is also another good indicator of the quality of a backlink. The higher the PR, the more weight that link carries. However, PR is quite volatile and is sometimes not very accurate because of the delayed updating. PR is actually updated constantly by Google's algorithm, but only updated every few months for the public so bear that in mind. To check a page's PR visit this website https://www.pagerank.net/pagerank-checker/ or use the SEOQuake extension tool.

Something absolutely crucial for you to know is **Domain Authority**. In simple terms, Domain Authority is a rank between 0-100 (0 = lowest, 100 = highest) that is given to your site's domain name. This rank is calculated by a measurement of your domain's **age.** A website that has been managed and updated over a longer period of time is seen as a trustworthy site. It also measures **popularity**, which includes backlinks, and finally your site's **size**, the amount of content, the length of that content and the number of pages your site has. These 3 factors are what make up your score and can be used to distinguish a 'powerful', authority site from weaker sites. As I just showed you, backlinks play a big part in your domain authority score and your domain authority score plays a role in your rankings. Backlinks from sites with high Domain Authority Ranks are much more powerful.

Another amazing factor is **Anchor Text**. Anchor texts are links that contain keywords relating to the site they are directing the user to. Instead of simply using a "Click-Here" link, use "Vegan Recipes Here" for example. By doing the latter, you would be telling the search engine what the content of that link is and subsequently giving yourself a nice boost. If you can have more links like this, with a variation of related keywords linking to your site, then your backlinks will be of higher quality. Just be sure to target the best keywords possible.

Remember: <u>Always</u> use your keywords, not you brand name unless the brand name is the keyword!

Search engines also value very highly **links that are included within the actual content**. This shows the search engine that the website that is linked, and is more important than links at the bottom of the website for instance.

The final point I will mention relates to one of the methods commonly used to acquire more backlinks: link exchanges. Now, doing link swaps will not get you nor your site in problems (unless done excessively) but, nowadays they are less impactful because they were overdone and eventually devalued by Google. Also, from a search engine's point of view, swaps are not real indications of a site's popularity.

For this reason, a higher quality link should come from website Example.com only and there should not be a link from your site that links to a website Example.com. However, this would contradict the purpose of a swap as you will be expected to also include a link on your own site. A clever way around this is to have a second site or a blog. What you do is contact the potential swapping partner and offer to link their site to your second website/blog, in exchange for a link from their site to your main website.

Nevertheless, my advice to you would be to not to focus too much on swaps as there are better methods to obtain links and traffic from other websites, which is what we will discuss next.

8 Awesome Ways to Obtain More Backlinks and Traffic

1. Social Media

Social Media is probably the most important vehicle not only for link building, but also for branding and marketing. Today, companies spend a lot of money advertising on social networks trying to establish their online presence and followers. It is also known amongst bloggers and internet marketers that social media can also boost your search engine ranking, but this is not always the case. Even though your social media profiles may not give you an instant ranking boost, you will certainly benefit indirectly.

I'll explain.

The major social media sites are some of the most visited sites in the world and Facebook is #1 making them not only highly trusted by Google and other search engines, but also extremely high authority sites when it comes to ranking on search results.

When you create a Facebook profile for example, you get automatically added to search engines and ranked highly for the keywords in your profile name. That means that your social profiles also rank very highly on search engine results without you doing much, making you "guilty by association". This is a lot of exposure for your content and your site and as time goes by, your following will increase. You will see a big difference in your rankings and traffic numbers. You just have to make sure that you leverage this advantage and put out great engaging content so that you may grow rapidly. We will discuss the importance of content more in the last chapter so do not miss it!

Now, when it comes to backlinks, you have to be clever about how you do it. To reduce spamming, many social networks include a 'no-follow' tag in their code that basically tells search engines that backlinks should not be created on their site. This small change led many to give up on the idea of using social media sites for link-building, but like that saying goes:

"Where there is a will, there is a way…"

The following are social media sites where you can build links, absolutely authorized by Google;

- **YouTube**- Besides being an amazing platform to increase exposure for your brand and to attract thousands, if not millions of new viewers, YouTube also allows you to link your site in your profile without a no-follow tag. This is a powerful backlink that will boost your rank, divert a lot of traffic and build your brand and reputation. A good strategy with YouTube is to create a video 'summary' of all your new blog posts, share it on your blog, other social profiles and watch your popularity grow. Use it and abuse it!

- **LinkedIn-** LinkedIn is a great way to build an authority brand, to connect to other people in similar industries and with similar interests, as well as draw awareness. Make sure you create a profile for yourself and one for your site/blog. When creating the profiles, you will have the option to enter your website link. Click *other* and it will allow you to select the text for your link (anchor text). It will also give you space for a second and third website link, use them all!

- **Google Profiles-** With Google Profiles, you can link all your social sites as well as your blog/website. The link has no 'no-follow' tag and you can also use anchor text for a highly optimized link. Use this medium to share content and build a relationship with your followers.

All the other social networking sites may have a 'no-follow' tag but they are still very important to have. Even if you are not getting a backlink from all your social profiles, it is still massive advertisement for your brand. As long as you are putting out engaging content and are making the effort to grow a social following, it will benefit you immensely in the near future. Even short-term, you will be getting shares, likes, views, traffic etc. which companies invest a lot of money to achieve.

Other Popular Social Media Sites You Should Definitely Consider

- **Facebook-** Build a page for your site and share every single step that you make on Facebook. Everything that you do on other social-networks including videos, photos, blog posts, etc., share them on Facebook. My advice here would be to post content on Facebook that people in your industry are interested in and may be searching for on search engines and do this on a regular basis. Remember, Facebook is the most popular website worldwide so make sure to put some focus on this platform.

- **Twitter-** Twitter is all about 'tweeting' and 'retweeting' content. Aim to tweet as much as you can, and follow and retweet the big players in your industry.

- **Instagram-** Now this one may not be for every market but if it is, take advantage of it. For instance, my 'Vegan Recipes' example would be perfect. I could share pictures of new recipes, get people to post pics of what they have cooked and link/hash tag to our profile, and we could even re-post their pics on our profile. People have a natural urge for recognition so use it in your favour! This is a great strategy to build the community feel and get people to want to engage. Mould it to fit your market.

- **Pinterest-** Pinterest is a great platform to also share your content as it is very easy to find on search engines and also encourages sharing. Users are able to 'pin' your posts on their boards and also share them with other users. Make sure you use it!

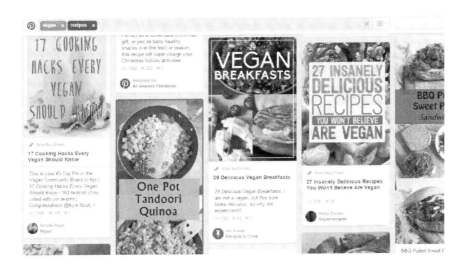

- **Google Plus-** Google + is an absolute must. It is like a cool blogging platform that is fun and can be easily optimized. The information that you include in your Google + posts is instantly indexed for Google search. I strongly recommend that you become as active as possible on Google Plus. Follow all the important and engaged people in your industry and take part in conversations, hangouts and contribute quality content. With Google +, you can add headlines that are used as title tags and displayed in the search result, which is very powerful. In addition to that, you can add links to all your posts and it will show a preview of your site in the actual post. That's very cool! You can also optimize your posts by using bolded text, bullet points, numbered lists and even hashtags, making your posts stand-out from the rest.

Here is how:

To create a bold headline: ***Write your Headline Here***

Italic text: _Italic_

Bold text: **Bold**

For a numbered list:
1 Text Here
2 Text Here
3 Text Here….

For Bullet points:
• Point 1
• Point 2
• Point 3

Hashtag posts: #Hashtag-here

Link: www.example.com

It will look like this on Google Plus;

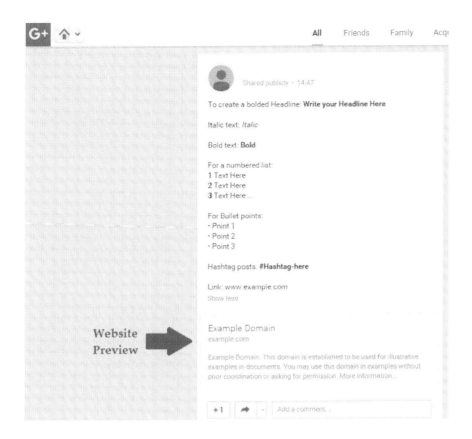

When creating posts on the social media sites I just discussed with you, make sure you include your website link in everything. Also, be sure to use the relevant keywords you are targeting in every single post and be sure to try out different headlines to see what gets the best clicking-rates.

Finally, link all your social profiles you create to your blog and site so that people can easily share your content, to do this simply visit www.addthis.com to install some awesome, free sharing buttons!

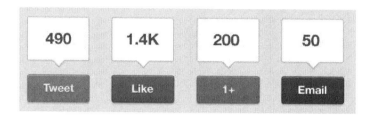

2.   Blogging

Blogging is vital. This is probably the best way to build a following, get traffic, promote your brand and rank high on search engines.

To me, the best way to blog is to create blog posts with **fresh content** that provide information, solve common problems and answers questions that the target market has. All the 'How to...? and 'Top 10...' and 'The best...', are all great ways to structure your posts. Make sure you research the most common issues and target the topics people are actually trying to get answers to. You can use the Google AdWords tool to find the best topics to write about.

The best sites for blogging:

- WordPress
- Blogger.com
- Weebly.com
- Penzu.com
- Typepad.com

I will also add that many people may use the excuse that they don't know how to write and so on. What I will say is that when you are blogging focus on the important task which is solving the reader's problem. Your writing skills will improve with practice. However, if you really hate writing, you can hire people to write for you. Sites like upwork.com have great freelance writers for really fair prices. You can even find quality writers to write 500 word posts for as little as $5 (fiverr.com). Another way is through guest blogging. There are many great people out there in your niche that would be happy to write great posts on your site in exchange for the permission to link to their own site in the post. The options are endless…

3. Guest Posting

Talking about guest blogging, you can also do posts on other people's sites and have your contributed content link to your site. Simply Google "[your-keyword] + guest post", or "[keyword] + guest writer", etc. or use http://myblogguest.com/ where you can find blog-owners looking for guest-writes and writers looking for blogs to share their content. Once you find a relevant site, contact the sites and tell them you will write fresh, free content if they allow you to link your site. This will save them time and money, and you will benefit from a backlink, some exposure and additional traffic. It's a win-win scenario.

4. Article Writing and Submitting

Article writing does work better in some markets than others, but it can still be a cool strategy to get more eyes on your content and as a way to build more backlinks. Similar to blogging, you want to target common topics in your market. Answer questions and provide new information. You can also use article writing to recycle older blog posts.

Be sure to optimize your articles well by including the proper keywords in your content, titles and subheadings. Also, include pictures for a more enjoyable reading experience.

Remember to include links to as many relevant posts on your blog and website.

Here are some of my favourite article submission sites:

- **EzineArticles.com** - Very popular submission site. It allows you to select a good number of keywords you want to target and you can also enter links in the *Resource Box.*
- **StumbleUpon.com** - Another popular site for article submission and also for social networking. You can actually share blog posts and pages and have them viewed and rated by viewers. It's really cool!
- **HubPages.com** - Awesome site. It will allow you to use anchor text for your links and is also free from the 'no-follow' tag.

Here is a useful list of the most popular article submission sites on the web. It will also have a small column that will tell you whether the site has a no-follow tag or not. Enjoy!
http://www.vretoolbar.com/articles/directories.php

5. Website Directories

Submitting sites to web directories is a very basic, but important step. Web directories are sites that store your page in their database and display them to users under specific categories.

One can simply go on Google and search "Web directories" and find numerous services where you can submit your site. However, my advice is to look for directory sites that target your particular market. Instead of simply searching for directories, add your keyword to the search.

For example, I Google searched "Link submission health and fitness" and web directory sites came up that are specifically for health and fitness.

Google   link submission health and fitness

Web   Images   Videos   News   Shopping   More ▾   Search tools

About 70,100,000 results (0.33 seconds)

Health and Fitness Directory - Submit Free Url
www.body-mind-strength.com/directory/**submit**.php ▾
Submit your free link to our **health and fitness** directory resource. All **links** are manually reviewed before acceptance.

Submit Link - Health Directory
www.**healthdirectorymoz**.com/**submit**.php ▾
5 Oct 2015 - **Health** Information · **Submit Link** ... First Aid · Fitness Websites · Health Administration · HEALTH INFORMATION ... Please send an email to infoAThealthdirectorymoz.com if you wish to suggest your health related resource.

Health and Fitness Link Exchange Directory - Facebook
https://www.facebook.com/**Health-and-Fitness-Link**-Exchange-Directory... ▾
Health and Fitness Link Exchange Directory. 2250 likes. Submit your site to the Health and Fitness Link Exchange Directory...

Health & Fitness Directory List - Directory Critic
www.directorycritic.com/**healthandfitness**-directory-list.html ▾
Promote your health and fitness related website by submitting it to these health ... 34; Jack Cole - Niche Health Links Directory; 1; 11-10-11; F, P; health-fitness ...

Submit Site - Health > Fitness - Submit url to Fitness Directory
www.argusvision.net › Health ▾
Search engine friendly **Fitness** web directory. Boost your search engine ranking in

Doing this will provide you with a higher quality backlink and also place your site in front of the appropriate viewer. Simply search: "Link submission + [keyword/niche]" or "web directories + [keyword/niche]".

6.   Local Listing

Another thing you can do is post your site on local listing sites. Some of these sites, like Google Places for instance, are easily found on search engines and allow you to attach links that are free from the no-follow tag.

Best Local listing sites:

- Google Places – www.google.com/business
- Foursquare – www.foursquare.com
- Yelp – www.yelp.com
- Yellow Pages – www.yell.com
- Yahoo Local – www.local.yahoo.com
- Bing Places – www.bingplaces.com
- InsiderPages – www.insiderpages.com
- SuperPages – www.superpages.com

7.   Forum Posting

Forums are still very popular. People use them to discuss things of interest and to ask questions that they may have. You can create your own forum discussions and engage with people in your target market, where you can provide value and promote your website and content. Some sites have a 'signature' box where you can include your website link, which can be crawled by search engines and give you an extra boost.

The best thing to do is to target forums that are related to your topic and have active community users that can be possible leads for you. Also, create posts that provoke engagement and sometimes posts that are positively controversial to get maximum input.

Finally, make sure you follow the important guidelines of the forum so you don't get penalized and also don't forget to always share your posts on your social profiles also in addition to bookmarking the page.

8.   Press Releases

Finally, the last strategy I will talk about are Press releases. Press releases are a great, inexpensive method that can create additional exposure for your site and brand. A press release is simply a statement sent to newspapers that informs them about a particular event. These statements can sometimes be picked up by big newspapers that will offer to feature you in their paper, interview you on radio shows, TV shows, podcasts, etc. It can really change a brand's success almost 'overnight'.

Even if you don't get massive attention like that, you are still likely to be shared on various sites and sources, giving you additional backlinks and traffic. If additional backlinks weren't good enough, many sites that get their hands on press releases are high quality and authoritative sites, meaning a greater quality link.

Now, I would recommend a small investment in this strategy simply because you cannot control whether your press releases are accepted by certain sites or not, so you don't want to make a huge investment. Unless you really have a super exciting thing to share with newspapers that they will be dying to get their hands on, then keep your costs down. You can get a good quality, 500-word press release written for you for $5 on Fiverr, you can also have your release submitted for you on tens of sites for also just $5 on Fiverr.

Remember to also optimize your statements and link your sites and social profiles for maximum publicity.

Awesome stuff! That was a great load of incredible information!

In the next chapter, we are going to talk about the importance of indexing and site-mapping a website. This so important, do not miss it!

Chapter Five: Index and Sitemap

Having an indexed website is a critical step in optimizing your site and getting it to rank high in search engine results for your keyword. By simply submitting your URL to search engines or using backlinks, you are technically only submitting the home page or one single page of your site. Having only one page in the search engines reduces your chances of achieving a really high ranking for a keyword, so increase your chances by having your entire site indexed.

A perfect way to get your website indexed is to submit a sitemap. A sitemap consists of an XML file that contains URLs of different pages and links on your site. Essentially, site-mapping your site will allow Google to properly crawl and index your website, getting <u>all</u> your content and pages available on Google. This is an important step to take if you wish to have the best SEO results.

Firstly, you can check and see what pages of your site have already been indexed. Just go to Google and search "site:YourURLHere.com". See what pages come up in the results. If you get no results, or not all of your important pages, it's time to submit your entire site.

It is advisable to have your website fully complete before submitting your website. Please complete the information from the previous chapters in its entirety before continuing.

We will use Google sitemap as the main example.

Creating a Sitemap

Here is how to create and submit your Sitemap. The first step is getting your site on the Google Webmaster Tool:

1. Visit www.google.com/webmasters/tools and login with your Gmail account.

2. Paste your URL in the box and click on *Add Property*.

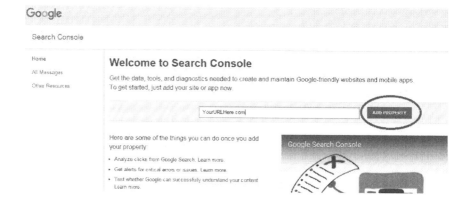

3. You should land on a verification page. Click on the *Alternate Methods* tab.

4. Select *HTML tag.*

5. Copy the metatag displayed.

HTML tag

Add a meta tag to your site's home page

1. Copy the meta tag below, and paste it into your site's home page. It should go in the <head> section, before the first <body> section.

<meta name="google-site-verification" content="..." />

100

WordPress Users (Coders, please skip!)

Now, if you are using WordPress, follow these instructions:

1. Go to your WordPress Dashboard. Hover over *SEO* and click on *General.*

2. Click on the *Webmaster Tools* tab.

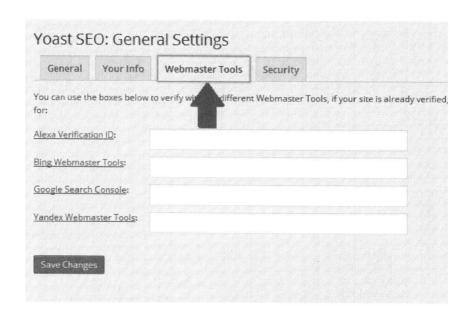

3. Paste the metatag in the *Google Search Console* box, but only keep the text between the quotation marks (after *'content='*).

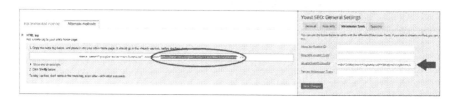

4. Click *Save Changes.*

5. Go back to the Google Webmaster site and click on *Verify* at the bottom of the page.

6. Once your site is verified, you want to click *Continue* and then return to the WordPress Dashboard.

7. Hover over *SEO* and click on *XML Sitemaps*.

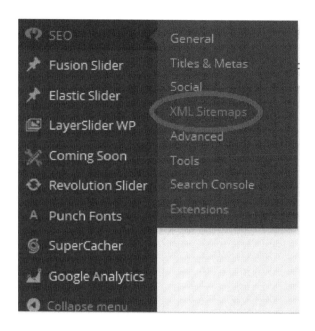

8. Check the following box:

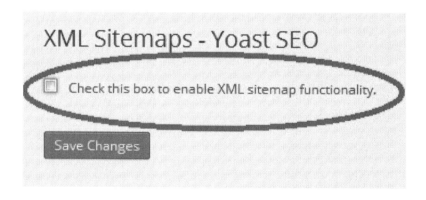

9. Click *Save Changes* to activate the XML sitemaps.

XML Sitemaps - Yoast SEO

☑ Check this box to enable XML sitemap functionality.

| **General** | User sitemap | Post Types | Excluded Posts | Taxonomies |

You can find your XML Sitemap here: XML Sitemap

You do **not** need to generate the XML sitemap, nor will it take up time to generate after publishing a post.

Entries per page
Please enter the maximum number of entries per sitemap page (defaults to 1000, you might want to lower th

Max entries per sitemap: 1000

Save Changes

10. A new set of options will show up, simply click on *XML sitemap* to view your sitemap. If you got a 404 error when trying to view your sitemap, go to your Dashboard, click on *Settings > Permalinks >* and click *Save Changes* without altering anything. Try again, and that should fix it.

11. The XML Sitemap should open in a new tab.

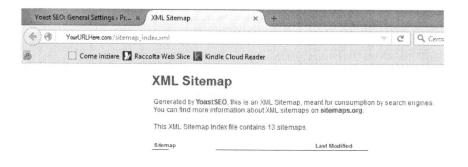

12. Copy the XML Sitemap URL (just the text after your domain-name).

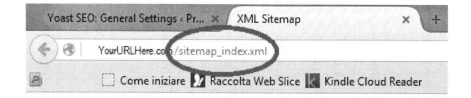

13. Go back to the Webmaster Tool and click on *Crawl*, then under that click *Sitemaps*.

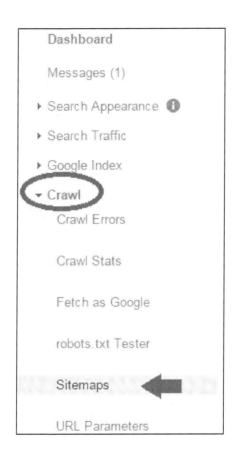

14. Click *Add/Test Sitemap* in the top right.

15. Paste the Sitemap URL.

16. Then you want to click *Test Sitemap* to verify everything is fine.

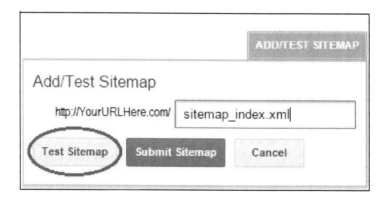

17. Once you get a confirmation that there are no errors, click *Add/Test Sitemap* again, paste the URL and finally click on *Submit Sitemap.*

18. Done!

Since you are using WordPress and Yoast SEO, you will not have to resubmit sitemaps since it will automatically update it for you. Also your new posts will be crawled by Google and your index updated within 1-4 days on average!

Sitemap submission is also quite similar for other search engines like Bing and Yahoo. For instructions on how to submit the site map, visit these links >> For Bing visit http://webdesign.about.com/od/sitemaps/ht/submit_sitemap_bing.htm - For Yahoo visit http://webdesign.about.com/od/sitemaps/ht/submit_sitemap_yahoo.htm.

Coding Masters (WordPress Users, please skip!)

Here are the instructions to generate your Sitemap:

1. Visit www.xml-sitemaps.com/

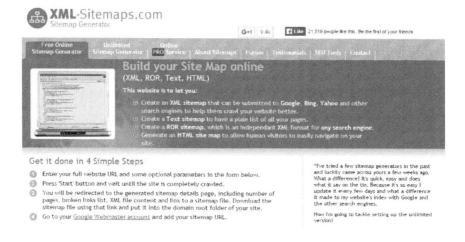

2. Enter your full URL in the box.

Starting URL

Please enter the **full** http address for your site, only the links within the starting directory will be included.

```
http://YourURLHere.com
```

3. Change frequency to *Always*.

4. *Last Modification* should be set to *Use Server's response.*

5. *Priority* should be set to *Automatically Calculated Priority.*

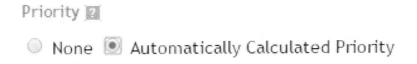

6. Click on the *Start* button.

Check your settings and click button below

Start | Maximum **500** pages will be indexed in sitemap

Need to index more? Check our Standalone version of Google sitemap generator with **unlimited** number of pages for crawler.

7. Your Sitemap should be ready for Download. Click the '*here*' link:

Your sitemap is ready!

There are 2 steps left:

1. Download the sitemap file here and upload it into the domain root folder of your site (http://www.solveinweb.com).

2. Check that sitemap is showing for you at http://www. YourURLHere.com/sitemap.xml, go to your Google Webmaster account and add your sitemap URL.

8. A file called *Sitemap.xml* should be saved. Add it to your desktop so it is easier to find.

9. Now go to your website host Control Panel. If you followed my instructions in the Word Press book (http://amzn.to/1VHtxZi), you should be using Bluehost. However, most hosts are quite similar so follow along:

10. Find your *File Manager*.

11. A 'File Manager Directory Selection' window should open, select *Web Root (Public_html/www)*- and Click '*Go*'. It should look something like this:

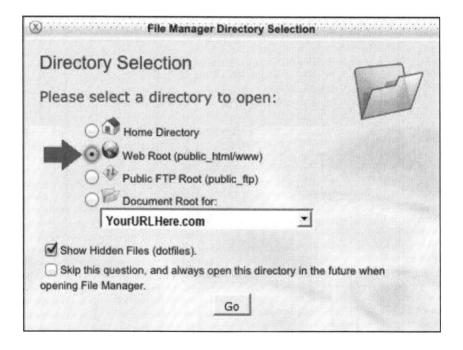

12. Now you want to click *Upload,* found on the top left of your host's File Manager- Choose File.

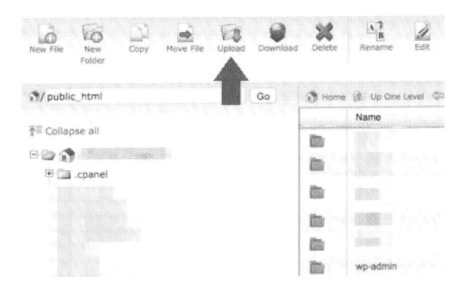

13. Find the *Sitemap.xml* File and upload it.

14. Once the sitemap uploading is complete, refresh the File Manager page and you should see the Sitemap.xml file in the files list.

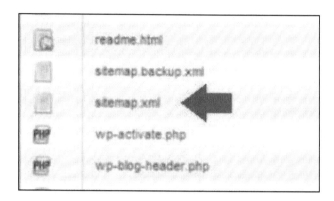

15. Now, let's quickly verify your site on Google Webmaster. Simply return to Google webmaster, and copy the full metatag from the HTML tag verification that I showed you previously

16. Now we need to paste that into your Home page's HTML, so open up Kompozer or the editor you use to edit your HTML. If you are using Kompozer, remember to click *source* at the bottom of the page to see the HTML code. Look for the *<head>* section of the HTML source and paste that tag in. It should look something like this:

116

```
           <html>
➡      <head>
            <meta name="google-site-verification"
                content="3LrMwkHbY2ST5CIqm-EcTNLtzU7lGCZuzDyCQ6f9COo" />
            <title>
                My fabulous homepage
            </title>
➡      </head>
           <body>
           <p>
               Lots of great content.
           </p>
           </body>
           </html>
```
Remember to paste the metatag between the <head> tags

<head> "paste here" </head>

17. Save your HTML code.

18. Now go back to the Webmaster tool and click
    Verify. Once complete, press *Continue* and
    return to the xml-sitemaps.com site.

19. Open up your Sitemap URL link.

Your sitemap is ready!

There are 2 steps left:

1. Download the sitemap file here and upload it into the domain folder of your *site* (http://www.solveinweb.com).
2. Check that sitemap is showing for you at http://www. YourURLHere.com/sitemap.xml, go to your Google Webmaster account and add your sitemap URL.

20. Copy the URL of the sitemap, but only the text the comes after '*.com/*'. Then return to the Webmaster Tool Dashboard, click *Crawl* then *Sitemaps.*

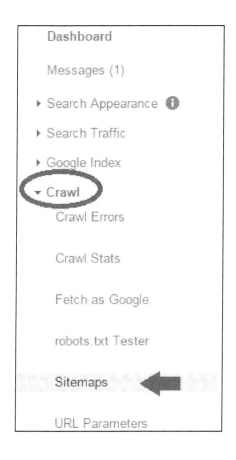

21. Press *Add/Test Sitemap,* paste the Sitemap URL and press *Test Sitemap.*

22. Once you see there are no errors, re-paste the URL and this time click *Submit Sitemap.*

23. Done!

Phew! Congratulations on getting through that. That is a massive step in your optimization process.

Webmaster Tool

I also want to make you aware that there is a lot you can do with Google's Webmaster tool. Here are a few cool features:

- Under '*Search Appearance*' you can:
  - Use *Data Highlighter* to tell Google about specific data on your page which you want to be highlighted (or displayed) in Google search results.
  - *HTML improvements* will detect any problems with your coding to see if there are missing or duplicate title or description tags.
  - And more!

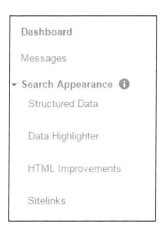

- Under '*Search Traffic*' you can:
  - *Search Analytics* will show your keyword and clicks data.

- See the *Links to your site*, and check all your backlinks to ensure everything is fine. It's a great tracking tool!
- Also *Internal Links* can be seen since it will show all the internal links you have and ensure they are working correctly.
- *Manual Actions* will show you whether there have been any manual attacks on your site.
- Use *International Targeting* to choose what the language and the country(ies) you want your website to target.
- And more!

- Under '*Google Index*' you can:
  - Check your Index Status
  - See what keywords are being used in your content
  - Remove particular URLs
  - And much more!

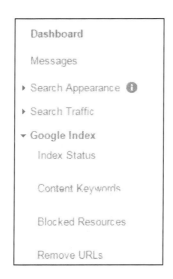

Finally, Google will also send you important data about your website such as any issues with security with your site, with your pages, etc. You will receive updates by email and in your Webmaster Dashboard.

And you are done! Now your site is indexed to have a greater chance of reaching that sky-high ranking! That's another big hurdle beaten and crossed! You're on your way to getting your site on the SEO throne. Give it a day or two to be completely submitted, then you can check again and see if it's been properly indexed by searching on Google using 'site:YourURLHere.com' as we did in the first part of this chapter. If you still don't receive results when checking for indexing double check your sitemap to make sure it was properly generated or contact Google to see if there was an internal problem with your site.

If you did not use WordPress to create your site or blog you will have to continuously revise and resubmit your sitemap whenever you make updates to your site, such as with a new page with new content. This way, all new pages will be available to search engines.

An easy way to do this is by using the *Fetch as Google* feature located under *Crawl* in your Webmaster Dashboard.

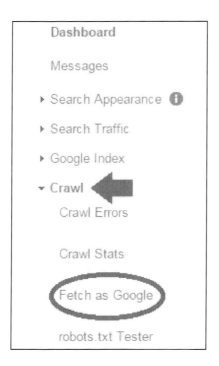

Please remember to not feel discouraged if after completing this you are not ranked right at the top. It will take some time to get everything submitted and approved before it's out there and even then, you may need to continue with optimization before you feel satisfied with your results. Optimization will always need to be checked and updated, so these past 2 chapters are crucial to follow correctly and to remember for future reference.

Now that we have optimized our site and indexed it for the utmost success on search engines, it's time to move on.

In the next and final chapter, I will discuss the importance of high-quality content in more detail and more importantly, I will teach you how to create content that is unique, engaging, and fresh and adds value to the reader. I will also touch on how to create content that encourages shares and likes on social media, so that you may grow your followers, get more traffic, links and simply take your site or blog to the next level.

Chapter Six: The Most Important Factor in SEO: Content

In this final chapter, I am going to talk about the most important factor in SEO: CONTENT. At the end of the day, no matter how many strategies you apply, no matter how many backlinks you acquire or even if you have great keyword research, if you're content is not good, you will not be successful long term.

What I have taught you so far, will bring you results, no doubt about that, but you will not reach a pinnacle if you are not providing the value to what your target market wants, sooner or later you will decrease in ranking or you will become stagnant.

The reasons for this are obvious. People will stop caring about what you have to say because you are not solving their queries. Another blog or brand may also see the gap in the market and provide the value the market wants and completely overtake you. In addition to that, if your content is not good people will simply bounce off your site, showing Google that you do not provide the answer people are looking for leading you to lose rank as time goes by. Google has done some major algorithm updates (Panda, Penguin) a few years back and us online marketers, saw that Google changed its focus to quality and has been tightening their algorithms more and more to ensure that only sites that meet their purpose are ranked high.

We have to understand that Google's main business is search results (Another business is ads of course.) and as they put it themselves,

"Our goal is to get visitors to the answer they're looking for faster, creating a nearly seamless connection between the visitor and the knowledge they seek".

From that statement alone, we can see that sites that follow Google's vision and purpose will be the ones to rank high, so our aim should be to provide people with solutions, with right information, to teach them the skill they require, to entertain them, and to give them <u>exactly</u> what they are looking for. This is what Google sees as quality content and this is what, combined with proper optimization, will get you to the top.

Focus on providing value to the viewer and build that trust and relationships with them and Google will reward you.

Now, there are a few things you need to know to do this correctly and I am going to break it down to you as simple as possible.

Understand the Market

First and foremost, if you want to give your market what it needs and wants, you need to understand them.

You need to have knowledge of what challenges they face!

Put yourself in the market's shoes and try to understand what their most common battles are. If you can discover this, you will be amazed by the growth, engagement and the following your blog and site will achieve. The more problems you solve for people and the more success you help them achieve, the more they will follow and promote you. It is like what I spoke about in my best-selling book *"EBay: Find All You Need to Sell on EBay and Build a Profitable Business from Scratch, Step-By-Step"* (http://amzn.to/1R1vnCP).

In that book, I spoke about the importance of asking yourself the right questions to ensure you truly understand the market you are selling to. You should be asking questions like:

- What doubts do they have?
- What challenges does my target market face?
- What questions are they asking?
- What skills do they want to learn?
- What do they like?
- What do they not like?

Answering simple questions like these will allow you to focus on particular issues to tackle. Aim to find the most popular problems, so that your audience may be larger and your efforts more effective.

Finding The Issues Your Market Has

- Emails and Comments

This is a big one. Many times you will receive messages from your readers and followers, or people that stumble on your post or site. These messages can contain questions that can be indicators of what answers your market is searching for. If there is a decent amount of people with the same query, take that opportunity and create a short blog post or video answering that question so that other people can also benefit from it. You could even do the classic "Dear John" style of answer (John is the name of the person that asked the question). This is not only quality content but also a good viewer experience. I will talk more about viewer experience shortly.

- Create a Survey

You can also create a survey for free using free tools like Surveymonkey.com. With Surveymonkey you can post surveys on your social media profiles, on your site, or even email them directly to your subscribers to get exact answers. This will be valuable information, coming directly from your market and describing exactly what interests them and what issues they have. You can do simple multiple answer questions, with a box for them to write more in-depth answers if they wish. The information you can gather from a simple

130

survey can really open your eyes and increase your understanding of your audience.

- ## Q&A Sites

You can also use 'Q&A' sites like Yahoo Answers, LinkedIn Answers, and Quora besides others, to find the most popular questions people are asking. These sites can be targeted by categories and topics so that you can find questions that are related to your market.

- ## Forums and Blogs in Your Niche

Go on forums and look through discussions. See what questions get the most views. You can also engage with some people to find out what their biggest challenges are.

Don't forget to also have a look around on your competitor's sites. I am not recommending that you steal their content, but get ideas. Go through the comments on their posts to see if there are any topics you can target. Look at FAQ's (Frequently Asked Questions) pages, as this is also a great place to find good topics to address.

Focus On the Market

This goes hand-in-hand with the point I made about understanding your market. You don't want to solely focus on your brand, your product and what you have to offer. Make it your goal to shift some of that focus to your target market. This may sound obvious, but many of us simply get caught up in focusing so much on our content and our aims that we forget that the answers are in the market. If we focus on the people we will discover what they need, what their questions/doubts are and in return will direct our efforts in the correct direction.

One of the best lessons I ever received when it comes to achieving success and recognition, is the formula:

VALUE=SUCCESS

The more value you provide to more people, the more success you will get in return. With that in mind, it is easier to understand a market's needs and provide them a solution (through your content, products and/or services) if you are targeting a specific group.

Target The RIGHT Keywords

Like we already discussed earlier in the book, keywords are a vital element for SEO success and when writing content, they are very important. When creating your high-quality content, you have to ensure that the people looking for the answers can find your material. Therefore, it is wise to do keyword research so that you may know exactly what terms your market is searching and rank for the best terms possible.

Besides knowing the right terms, doing keyword research can also provide you with other topics to target. It can give you ideas and it can show you the true demand for a particular query. To do this, simply use the Google AdWords Tool, but be sure to narrow your search down to a particular geographic location so that the data may be accurate for the location of your target market. Also, play around with the different filters to get more ideas and don't focus solely on popularity, as there may be some good opportunities for terms that are a little less popular. If there is a term with 1,000 monthly searches, for instance, and there is no real competition for that term, then that is a great term to rank for as you will easily hit the number one spot.

Remember: Creating quality content is usually providing 'free' information and not selling anything. If you have a site mainly devoted to selling products or services, then you want to target buying keywords. These keywords will be the best words for you to rank for as you will be giving people with buying intent exactly what they are looking for. I would still produce information providing free content as this will direct more traffic to your site, but your main focus should be those buying keywords.

Finally, it is important to be aware that Google does not only judge the content of a site based on the *primary* keyword. Google looks at the entire content to find words that relate to each other to truly rank the site for that specific topic. Google has become so advanced and so intelligent that it accesses context. It looks for words known as 'proof terms' which are words that are usually included in posts on a particular topic. It also looks for 'relevant terms', which are words that are not as common but still relate to a sub-topic of the main topic you are targeting. This does not mean that you should 'keyword stuff'. That is the worst mistake you can make. Instead, focus on the topic of your post and do not divert to irrelevant areas.

Creating Great Content

Now, we will discuss the actual creation of content.

Create content that resonates with your viewer

Basic components to creating high quality content are perfect spelling and grammar, correct formatting and an aesthetically attractive layout. Failing to pull those off correctly will negatively affect your rank and simply make you look unprofessional and untrustworthy to viewers.

In addition to that, you need to deliver content that resonates with your consumer, content that really fits their purpose and is written in their 'language'. By this, I mean making the content easy for the viewer to follow and comprehend. If it is a complex subject or something that may be new to your market, try to approach it in a way that makes it clear and simple for your reader, explaining things in detail and avoiding jargon terminology.

A good way to make things easy to follow, is by creating content in a step-by-step format, allowing the viewer to follow each step at their own pace and making it easier for them to digest the information.

Create Attractive Posts

To this day, the most popular posts contain one of the following titles:

"How to…"

"Top 10…"

"5 Ways to…" etc.

These type of posts are great because they allow you to break things down into small chunks for readers to easily process, instead of going with the long essay post. Writing posts like 'Top 10' lists, grabs people's attention. You just have to ensure that your posts are well structured, in an organized order and are easy to follow.

To maximize the potential of this strategy, make sure your headline is strong. Headlines are a big factor in the number of clicks a post gets. Statistics from CopyBlogger.com, a very popular site for web marketers, has proven that 80% of people actually read your headline but only 20% will actually read the rest of your content. So the better the headline, the more people you can get to read your content.

Here are Some Quick Tips for an Effective Headline:

1. Again, use numbers if applicable such as 5 ways, 10 tips, etc.
2. Use trigger words like Why, How, When, What, etc.
3. Use your relevant keyword.
4. Use unique rationale like Tips, Ideas, Lessons, Secrets, Ways etc.

5. Use powerful adjectives such as Amazing, Best, Essential, Incredible, Important, etc.

For Example, you could have a post titled:

"5 Tips on How to Write Amazing Blog Posts"

or

"Writing Amazing Blog Posts: 10 Incredible Secrets" (Keyword closer to the front of the title)

Try different strategies to see what best resonates with your market.

Now onto the meat of the content itself.

5 Crucial Content Creation Steps

1. Use Media

Include images, infographics (information and data displayed in a diagram/image instead of just text) and videos in your posts. They make your material much more enjoyable to read and also boost your ranking on search engines. Besides user experience and ranking boosts, a test run by buzzsumo.com showed that content containing images got as much as 2 times the amount of social profile shares. Another study showed that videos were shared 12 times more than images and text put together, proving that media has a huge impact on social engagement! I will go into more detail into engagement in a second.

2. Be Innovative

Aim to make your content different and unique. By unique, I mean content that does not appear anywhere else, or at least not easily found all-over the internet. If you are able to find topics to target that are not being ranked for, then this is the easiest way to achieve maximum uniqueness, but don't worry too much about this.

If you are targeting a topic that is pretty common, but an important topic for you to target, don't try to reinvent the wheel. Aim to present it better than what is already out there. Take what has been done and think of creative ways you can deliver the message. Are there any major pieces missing? Can you deliver it in a more 'fun' manner? (ex: an animated video or comic approach) Can you deliver it in a way that is easier to understand?

3. Go into Detail

Whenever you are offering information, aim to do it to its fullest. Cover all key areas and ensure that the reader truly gains the knowledge they desire.

Also be aware that if you are writing articles, blog posts or any written material, it is important to pay a little attention to the length of your copy. A survey by SearchMetrics.com (leading site for SEO marketing analytics) found a connection between lengthier content and higher rankings. Their study revealed that the sites ranking highest on search engines had posts in their site with longer word lengths than sites further down the search results. Other authority sources have also backed this up. Content length has also been proven to play a part in social media shares (Source: buzzsumo.com) as there is more value being offered, more relevant keywords, more images, more links and so on. However, don't force the word count and be natural.

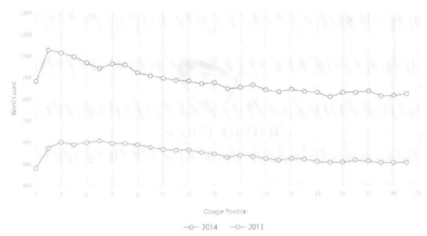

Word-Count vs Google Position survey (SearchMentrics.com)

4. Social Sharing and Viewer Engagement

Speaking about social shares, another study done by SearchMetrics.com found that posts that ranked on the highest positions on Google, tended to have larger numbers of social shares. Even though it has not been proven for sure that social shares alone boost rankings, it has definitely been shown through this study that 'social signals' have a massive impact on traffic numbers, brand image, recognition as well as your domain's overall performance. Don't forget to include social sharing buttons on your site and blog like I advised you in an earlier Chapter and most importantly; ask for shares, likes, comments, etc. Like one of my favourite *sayings* goes:

"Don't ask, Don't get…"

Asking people to share is asking them to engage and take action. You should take the same approach when introducing them to products and services you have or even other related posts. Tell them for example, "Click Here to Learn About Our Training Course". This simple shift will improve your conversions and will help you achieve your desired results. Don't be afraid and always include a call to action.

Always ask the readers for their feedback. Whether that is asking them what they thought about the topic, or even better, asking them to contribute their ideas in the comment section. For example:

"Can you think of any other ideas that may…? Make sure you share your wisdom in the comment section!"

Ending a post like that will encourage people to comment as they will feel like they are contributing. People love to feel important!

5. Optimize Correctly

If you are using WordPress (which I would recommend), the Yoast SEO plugin should keep you on track. Like we discussed you need Keywords in titles, Header tags, content, URL and images are your most crucial steps. Even if you are not using WordPress, make sure you optimize correctly how I have taught you in the previous chapters.

Also, link to sites where the reader can find more valuable information about what they are reading. This will boost user experience and increase the value. Besides outgoing links, include links throughout your content that link to other related topics and products on your own site.

Deliver The Content CORRECTLY

Now, the majority of this Chapter has been more focused on written content. However, I definitely urge you to use different media routes for content creation. It is important to understand that you have to deliver content in the best format for the market, whether that be written, or by videos alone, images, emails etc.

You have to again, understand your market a little more and have an understanding of their preferred way of digesting information. As you produce more and more content, your understanding of this will increase over time. After tracking the market's responses (very important!), you should see a pattern in what converts well, what gets most clicks, views, shares, etc. and this will tell you what to focus the majority of your attention on.

Run little experiments with your content where possible. Turn your content into a video, a blog post, as an email campaign and see what kind of result you get.

Common Vehicles for Content Delivery:

- Blog Articles
- Social Media posts
- Video posts
- Infographics/Image posts
- Email marketing
- Podcasts
- Webinars
- Case studies
- Guides

Finally, you can also ask your market what they like. Use the surveys I mentioned before and post them on social media, send emails, post them on your site and simply ask people what they prefer. Ask them:

"How do you like to view content?", and give them options; Videos, Blog Posts etc.

That is how to produce high quality content.

Congratulations! You are now well educated about SEO and have gained the knowledge you need to get your site high up in the rankings and to drive a lot of traffic your way. Of course, this is a continuous process, but you now understand the steps clearly and will be able to make great decisions and achieve massive success. I advise you to take action right away if you have not, and always return to this book if you need to refresh your mind about a particular step.

Turn to the next page for a quick recap of what we covered in this book!

Here is a quick recap of what we covered in case you need a refresher on a certain step:

1. You now have a good understanding of what SEO is and how it works
2. You also understand how search engines operate
3. You learnt how to correctly submit your site to search engines
4. You learnt about the importance of keywords
5. You learnt about the different variation of keywords (short tail vs long tail) and now have a full understanding of what keywords to target
6. You know how to find the most suitable keywords
7. You learnt how to manoeuvre Google AdWords like a pro
8. You also learnt how to carefully analyse the competitiveness of a term
9. You learnt how to optimize your site on-page
10. You learnt about Title Tags and how to create them
11. You learnt about Header Tags and how to add them to your site
12. You learnt about Meta Tags and how to create great Meta Descriptions
13. You know how to use URL's, images and links to better optimize your site for keywords
14. You learnt how to set up Google Analytics to track valuable data about your site's performance
15. You learnt how to optimize your site off-page

16. You learnt about the power of backlinks and you are knowledgeable about what makes a high-quality backlink
17. You learnt how to use Social Media, Blogging, Guest Posting, Article Writing, Web Directories, Local Listing, Forums and Press Releases to optimize your site, drive a lot of traffic and build high-quality backlinks
18. You learnt about the use of indexing and sitemaps
19. You now know how to generate sitemaps and how to submit the sitemap correctly
20. You learnt about the importance of high-quality content
21. You now know how to provide great value to your market by solving their problems/teaching them new skills and so on
22. You learnt about how to better understand your market
23. You learnt how to create awesome content that is engaging, unique and valuable to your market
24. And a lot more!

Wow! Just look at the skills you have attained by reading this guide. I really hope that you have found the knowledge you were looking for and this guide was worth every penny invested.

Turn to the next page see my other best-selling books part of this series!

Before You Go

I hope you have enjoyed this book and have benefited immensely from reading it. I made it my goal to offer value -and to give you the skills you require to rank your site highly on search engines, drive tons of traffic to your site and achieve great success. I am glad that you are reading this far down.

I would also really appreciate your reviews and your feedback. If you really enjoyed this book, then feel free to share it so other people may also profit from this information.

Please visit http://amzn.to/1NcHQkL to leave a review!

Here Are Other Books Our Readers Loved!

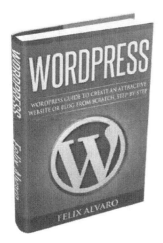

#1 Best Seller in Web Site Design

Easily Create Your Own Eye-Catching, Professional Website or Blog Using WordPress Today!

★★★★★

http://amzn.to/1VHtxZi

#1 Best Seller in Mathematical Set Theory

Learn JavaScript Programming Today With This Easy Step-By-Step Guide!

★★★★★

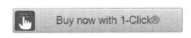

http://amzn.to/1mBhUYM

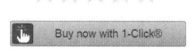
Best Seller in Popular Counting & Numeration

Learn Python Programming Today With This Easy, Step-By-Step Guide!

★★★★★

Buy now with 1-Click®

http://amzn.to/1WOBiy2

NEW

Learn Java Programming Today With This Easy, Step-By-Step Guide!

★★★★★

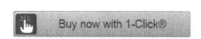
Buy now with 1-Click®

http://amzn.to/1WTgUw0

Learn The Linux Operating System and Command Line Today!

★★★★★

Buy now with 1-Click®

http://amzn.to/1QzQPkY

Launch Your Own Profitable eBay Business- Learn Everything You Need to Know to Get Started Today!

★★★★★

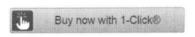
Buy now with 1-Click®

http://amzn.to/1R1vnCP

Learn C Programming Today With This Easy, Step-By-Step Guide

★★★★★

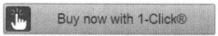

http://amzn.to/1Wl6fHu

Learn R Programming With This Easy, Step-By-Step Guide

★★★★★

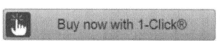

http://amzn.to/24XxoLM

150

Learn AngularJS
Web-App Developing
Today With This Easy,
Step-By-Step Guide

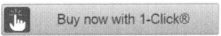

Buy now with 1-Click®

http://amzn.to/1pDq0BZ

Finally, you can also send me an email if you have any questions, feedback or just want to say hello! (I do reply!) My email address is; (Felix_Alvaro@mail.com)

I thank you once again and God bless!

Felix Alvaro

Printed in Great Britain
by Amazon